Thank you for;

# Tales Of Sheringham's Level Crossing

David Madden

Photographs by
Brian Fisher

Additional pictures and created images by
David Madden

authorHOUSE®

*AuthorHouse™ UK Ltd.*
*500 Avebury Boulevard*
*Central Milton Keynes, MK9 2BE*
*www.authorhouse.co.uk*
*Phone: 08001974150*

*First published by AuthorHouse 7/31/2009*

*ISBN: 978-1-4490-0354-8 (sc)*

*This book is printed on acid-free paper.*

# CONTENTS

# FOREWORD

By David Morgan MBE, TD,
*Chairman: North Norfolk Railway Plc.*

This book outlines the history of Sheringham's Level Crossing which was opened in 1887 and lifted in the early 1970's. Apart from the early history explaining how the crossing came to be built, David Madden has described how the setting up of the North Norfolk Railway at Sheringham prolonged its life after trains from the national network ceased to use the original station built in 1887. The timing of the publication of this book is particularly apposite, coming, as it does, when it seems that our partners' funding for the reinstatement of the crossing is more or less in place, although the North Norfolk Railway Plc needs to raise more.

Level crossings do, of course, have a special attraction for many people as it is often the closest individuals will get to trains other than on a raised platform. Because they are observing the train from the track level, watchers of the passage of a passing train will receive the full impact of its majesty as it towers above them.

Hopefully, this experience will be re-created in the near future, albeit on an occasional basis when special trains visit the North Norfolk Railway, and once again visitors to the town will be able to enjoy the sight of trains crossing Station Road to access our tracks. As the Railway's Chairman, I would like to thank the authors for their generous gesture in donating all the profits from the sales of this book to the fund we are raising to help pay for the reinstatement of this level crossing.

# Author's Notes

The railway level crossing at Sheringham between the current terminus, in fact a small halt, and the North Norfolk Railway –a thriving tourist steam railway – was removed some 33 years ago. This book tells the story of that level crossing and the aspirations of joining up the two railways once again.

The North Norfolk Railway (NNR) has long had a vision of seeing the two lines reconnected so that charter trains bringing more tourists to Sheringham could operate. (Tourist charter trains are a very rare sight at Sheringham – just two in over thirty years!). Locomotives and other rolling stock could be transferred by rail rather than road. The small Network Rail halt is incapable of handling anything longer than two-car trains, the norm on the regular service between Norwich and Sheringham.

Network Rail and the local authorities now agree that reconnecting the two railways is very desirable on an occasional rather than a regular basis. As the former General Manager I was involved in the railway almost from day one. The gap between the North Norfolk Railway and the national network was a tantalising 300 yards, one day that gap would be bridged. I was fortunate in being present on each occasion the crossing was used. This book is a tribute to British Rail (as they were then) and the countless numbers of volunteers who made these crossings possible. In writing this account I am especially grateful to Brian Fisher who, since the early days has kept a meticulous photographic record of all events on the railway. Without this record it is unlikely that this book could have been written.

# Chapter 1. Introduction.

The Eastern & Midlands Railway (E&MR) reached Sheringham in June 1887 as part of an extended line from Holt to a new terminus station at Cromer. This line functioned as a west-to-east cross country main line in opposition to the much larger Great Eastern Railway which had opened its line from Norwich to Cromer (later renamed Cromer High station) in 1876. The Eastern & Midlands Railway changed its name to the Midland & Great Northern Joint Railway, often known by its initials 'M &GN', this being more representative of the parent companies of the E&MR made up of the large Midland and the Great Northern Railways. They were looking to expand their influence into East Anglia which at that time was dominated by the Great Eastern Railway Company.

Sheringham was actually two villages; Upper Sheringham, the original settlement, was mainly a farming community whilst Lower Sheringham developed later as a fishing community. The arrival of the M &GN Joint Railway in 1887 provided a direct link with London via South Lynn and Peterborough, a journey which took about four hours. This gave Sheringham a two-fold advantage. Crabs and lobsters caught in the morning could be in London later that same day. Middle class Londoners discovered the quaint fishing town and as a result fishermen rented out their cottages to visitors. They found that they could earn more money in the summer than they could from the sea in a whole year.

In 1901 Lower Sheringham was granted status as a self governing urban district and the town of Sheringham was born, now boasting a population of over 7000.

Although the M&GN and Great Eastern railways were fierce rivals competing for traffic particularly to Cromer, the two railways gradually acknowledged each other. The Great Eastern's opening of its own office at Sheringham station thus provided a more direct route to London for the townspeople and goods. Further co-operation resulted in a joint venture to provide a new line through 'Poppyland' to Mundesley and thence joining the Great Eastern at North Walsham; this was completed in 1906

Train services grew with the development and popularity of Sheringham and Cromer. Sheringham station was a rather commodious station with both main platforms covered by extensive canopies. Sheringham had one signal box – a lofty structure on platform 2. The growth of rail traffic and, just as important the growth of road traffic which crossed the line at the eastern end of the station, meant that the signal box was replaced by two signal boxes known as 'East' (also controlling the level crossing) and 'West' (responsible for the carriage siding and trains to and from Melton Constable.) .

The closure of the former M&GN line through Fakenham, South Lynn and westwards in 1959 resulted in Sheringham being left with largely local trains eastwards to Cromer and Norwich and a short lived service westwards to Melton Constable, the latter closing in 1964. The result was that Sheringham's rather large station was now the terminus of a branch from Norwich via Cromer and each train needed to cross Station Road twice. It was inevitable that changes would be made and that Sheringham station would be closed in favour of a simpler station, in fact a rather short halt on the other side of the road.

On January 1st 1967, train services from Norwich to Sheringham terminated at the new halt on the Cromer side of Station Road. The then fledgling North Norfolk Railway through the Midland & Great

Northern Joint Railway Society had taken over the care and maintenance of the larger station. Their plans for re-opening the line towards Melton Constable meant its isolation from the national railway system in spite of the fact that the railway track across Station Road, the level crossing gates and the controlling signal box remained in place. However, all indications were that this link would be removed with the gates and signal box demolished.

This seemed to be the end of trains crossing Station Road into the larger station, probably much to the relief of road traffic. Demolition of the signal box and removal of the level crossing gates was to take time unlike the methods by which the track and buildings were hurriedly demolished. This delay provided opportunities for the level crossing to be used again with non-passenger special trains bringing locomotives and rolling stock from various storage locations for the established and rapidly developing North Norfolk Railway based at the old station in Sheringham.

The idea of re-instating the level crossing is not new. Indeed from the very beginnings of the North Norfolk Railway there were aspirations to retain the link with British Rail. However this was not to be as the local authority wanted to change the road layout by removing the level crossing completely. This was to take time however as you will see as the story unfolds.

As the North Norfolk Railway developed and privatisation of the national system was planned a great deal of work behind the scenes had been devoted to this very subject. It was a project which needed a lot of careful consideration and, perhaps not surprisingly, there was little comment from the company during this early discussion period. However, Norfolk County Council issued press reports on the subject, what was called a new "Partnership Agreement" for the Norwich to Sheringham line, so the NNR released details of these developments.

The Railways Act 1993 - the Act that made railway privatisation possible (and depending on which politician you listen to and believe in), meant that our railway system would grow and be more efficient and profitable, or enter a steady decline with about half of the lines closing within ten years! My own personal view at that time was that the new private operating companies would want to concentrate their efforts on the profitable operations, particularly the main lines. They might find the continued operation of branch lines such as Norwich to Sheringham an ever increasing burden, with little or no funds available for investment. It might have gone further with a demand that if the line is socially necessary for the area then the local authorities, through which such lines pass, might be asked to pick up the bill.

Our thinking at that time was that the survival of the Norwich to Sheringham line was vital for the communities and tourist industries of North Norfolk but, if the worst were to happen and the Norwich to Sheringham line closed, the North Norfolk Railway has always made it clear that it would be seriously interested in extending its services at least to Cromer. Chasing a closed line to North Walsham or indeed Norwich has never been a serious ambition. Fortunately none of this happened and the Sheringham line prospered.

Clearly, though it was in our interest to see the Sheringham line continue and prosper, we were delighted to hear that Norfolk County Council had commissioned consultants to examine ways and means of promoting the use of the line. The NNR had long discussions with the consultants and examined a number of roles that the North Norfolk Railway could play in any development plans. What was suggested in the subsequent report from the consultants was for there to be a Partnership Agreement with Railtrack (now Network Rail), the train operating companies, the local authorities and other interested bodies, North Norfolk Railway, of course, being included. The aims of the Partnership Agreement were clearly to establish ways and means ofpromoting the line, but we went much further and suggested that there were other opportunities worthy of exploration. We looked into several areas:

(a) We should examine re-instatement of the link between the two railways. If and when the link was re-instated, the local train operator might be interested in stabling the first and last trains of the day on the North Norfolk Railway. These first and last trains, whilst service trains, run largely as empty coaching stock in positioning moves. At the same time questions were raised about running all the national services into the NNR station; in the end this proved too expensive.

(b) We also examined the possibility of running off-peak services between Sheringham and Cromer providing an enhanced half-hourly summer service between the two resorts, with a further possibility of constructing new halts to directly serve caravan sites along the line.

(c) Of course, the re-instated crossing would allow occasional steam hauled trains from the national system. Unfortunately this is no longer a relatively simple operation as there are now no run-round facilities at Cromer, or room to build such within the station area. This was also not feasible at the time but the current plans of the NNR mean that occasional charter trains (extinct after the level crossing closure) would return to the benefit of both Cromer and Sheringham.

The re-instatement of the level crossing is perhaps the most important and emotive issue. Even during our discussions with the highway authorities it was clear that the traditional type of crossing with either gates or barriers was far too expensive. This was when we suggested what might be a more acceptable solution through the construction of a tramway type track without any barriers or fencing. The new link tastefully paved would be hardly noticed and would serve its purpose. The down side is that there would be restrictions on the operation of trains over the tramway. The time honoured method of a man walking in front with a red flag might be necessary! Preliminary talks took place with HM Railway Inspectorate and the highways authority and initial discussions were positive. So the seeds were sown.

The M & GN Society, formed to preserve and operate part of the closed section of the M & GN, had purchased two steam locomotives from British Rail (an 0-6-0 Class J15 No. 65462 and a 4-6-0 Class B12 No.61572). Both locomotives had spent most of their working lives in East Anglia. Whilst the initial stages of securing and reopening the now closed section of the line between Sheringham and Melton Constable were taking place, the locomotives languished in various locomotive depots in the London area but were finally stored at March locomotive shed in Cambridgeshire. Also acquired was a former Great Eastern Railway passenger coach. Another company had also been formed to become the operator of the proposed line from Sheringham to Melton Constable. There were legal reasons for the formation of a limited liability company in addition to the M & GN Society. The company also purchased a four-car set of articulated suburban wooden bodied coaches which had been withdrawn after carrying countless thousands of commuters to and from London. British Railways had been experimenting with simple railbuses built by Wagon & Machinbeau in Germany as a means of operating lightly used branch lines. Unfortunately the branch lines did not survive but the railbuses did and two were purchased around the same time. Clearly, it was time to transfer the locomotives and rolling stock to Sheringham.

*Early photograph of Sheringham station showing
the lofty signal box on platform 2.*

*Another early photograph of Sheringham Station showing the signal
box on Platform 2 taken from the former goods yard. (Unknown)*

*Sheringham Station from the air in 1968: David Madden*

*The opening of the halt in 1967 where all trains from
Norwich and Cromer would terminate.*

# CHAPTER 2.

*Train No. 1: 4th June 1967. 09.00 Wensum Sidings
(Norwich) to Sheringham, Special Freight Train.*

On the 4th June 1967 a train known simply as the 09.00 Wensum
to Sheringham Special Freight Train was booked to leave Norwich
(Wensum Sidings). This train, which was hauled by a Brush Class 31
diesel locomotive consisted of the two steam locomotives ex-March;
the four articulated coaches of the historic suburban set known as the
'Quad-Arts'; the former Great Eastern Railway passenger coach, and the
two German-built railbuses which had been stored at Wymondham.
British Rail needed persuading for the vehicles to be moved by rail but
accepted the need as it was quite impossible for the 4-car articulated
Quad-Art set to travel by road as each coach shared the bogies of
the other. Some time after 10.30 on Sunday 4th June the special
freight train arrived at Cromer (Beach) station where much shunting
was to take place to get the train in the right order to travel in the
opposite direction to Sheringham. It was necessary for the heavy steam
locomotives (the J.15 and B12) to be at the front and the lightweight
railbuses at the rear. All this took time and was the reason why Sunday
morning was chosen as, fortunately, timetabled passenger trains did
not commence until the afternoon.

At Sheringham the signal box which had been placed in the temporary care of the North Norfolk Railway was the movement's operational centre. Although it no longer controlled trains the gates could still be worked mechanically by the gate wheel in the signal box. Word travelled fast and by this time quite a crowd had assembled on Station Road as the Brush Diesel-Electric locomotive was sighted hauling the special train. Under the supervision of a British Rail Inspector the gates were opened for the first time since the closure. As it happened the gates were then closed again as the local police thought the train was far enough away for road traffic to continue crossing the line! The British Railways Inspector politely but firmly insisted that the gates must be opened in advance of the train's arrival.

The North Norfolk Railway was soon to see its first real train entering the station, although it would still be some time before NNR passenger train services could commence. The special train crossed the line and the BR locomotive helped to shunt the various vehicles into the old carriage sidings before departing over the crossing back to Cromer and Norwich. The operation was witnessed by hundreds of people, and also covered by the press with the BBC and ITV filming the whole operation. The level crossing gates closed again perhaps for the final time.

*Sheringham signal box in use for the first time in preparation for its first train since closure of the western section of the line*

*British Rail engineers removing the buffer stop and adding plain line rails in the gap for the June 1967 special train. Note lack of high visibility clothing.*

*Train No.1 pauses at Sheringham (Halt) before crossing Station Road.*

*The British Rail Class 31 diesel-electric locomotive, with the steam locomotives and coaches for the North Norfolk Railway, crosses Station Road.*

*The locomotives and coaches are shunted in the NNR sidings at journey's end.*

*The Gresley Quad-Art set and two diesel railbuses which formed part of the train from Norwich to the North Norfolk Railway.*

*Society members and the public take an interest in the B12 and J15 Locomotives after arrival.*

# CHAPTER 3.

*Train No.2: 24th April 1969 0950 Wensum Sidings (Norwich) to Sheringham, Special Freight Train.*

It may have been generally assumed that the special train described above would indeed be the last to cross the road. The reason was that the need for bringing locomotives and rolling stock by rail was considerably reduced as heavy-load haulage contractors were developing expertise in conveying rail vehicles by road. It was also much cheaper than by rail. Two factors changed this and created the need for a second special train; firstly, the level crossing, its gates and signal box were still in place and secondly, Wymondham Station was a temporary home for hundreds of redundant coaches most of them wooden bodied. 'Kings' scrap yard was situated on the nearby closed Forncett branch line where the coaches were simply set on fire leaving just the scrap metal. This was at a time when British Rail dispensed with many hundreds of coaches and the writer remembers seeing a group of Pullman dining cars in the sidings having only recently been taken out of traffic. Such was the hurry to break them up, one dining car still had its tables set for the last meal served!

Readers may ask what this has to do with the Sheringham level crossing. John Rumens, a Society member living at Wymondham, took a great interest in the movements there and particularly those vehicles heading towards the Forncett branch scrap yard. John had spent the last eighteen months of his time looking after the historic articulated Quad-Art set and the two diesel railbuses before they were transferred to Sheringham. During one of his many visits to the scrap lines John discovered two historic coaches in the sidings lined up for burning. These were a former Director's Saloon of the London & North Western Railway and a similar saloon formerly of the Lancashire & Yorkshire Railway. It would have been a tragedy for these to have been destroyed and soon they were acquired by the M&GN Society to be part of the growing collection. Both vehicles were safely recovered from the scrap lines and stored in private sidings at Wymondham. In addition the first of a number of steel-bodied coaches known officially as 'Tourist Second Open' or 'TSO' for short had been acquired; this was the first of many TSOs used on the North Norfolk Railway.

What altered the situation was that British Rail wanted to rationalise the track at Wymondham and road hauliers (at that time) could not offer economical transport of the twelve-wheeled LNWR saloon. Another problem was that there was no suitable road access to load the vehicles so some rail movements were inevitable. British Rail agreed that another special freight train could be run to travel to Sheringham over the level crossing.

The second special train was actually two trains; the first from Wymondham to Norwich and the second, a few days later, from Norwich to Sheringham. The train arrived at Cromer where it was only necessary for the locomotive to run round the train (still possible then). After the short journey to Sheringham the gates opened across the road for the second time. Then the British Rail class 31 Diesel-Electric locomotive hauled the coaches onto the North Norfolk Railway. The locomotive then ran round them via the loop line outside the west end of Sheringham station and quickly departed back to Norwich. This surely would be the last time the crossing was to be used. Not quite, as you will learn later on.

Incidentally readers may wonder how the buffer stop was removed and how the gap was filled with plain line. A small team of British Rail permanent way men were sent to each of the two jobs and manhandled the buffer stop to one side with nothing more than crowbars and rollers. Two special lengths of rail of an exact fit lay alongside the buffer stop ready for future movements!

*For the second time British Rail Engineers remove the buffer stop
and replace it with plain line rails for Special Train No.2.*

*Special train No.2 with additional coaches passes Sheringham*
*East Signal Box ready to enter the NNR station.*

*The Special Train arrives at the North Norfolk*
*Railway station with the new coaches.*

*Many visitors and residents witnessed the new arrivals and were able to make a close inspection from the platform at their new home.*

*Having finished its shunting duties, the Class 31 starts its journey back to Norwich via the level crossing.*

*The train movements were filmed by the BBC providing much publicity for the North Norfolk Railway.*

# CHAPTER 4.

*Train No. 3: 09.00 16th March 1975 - Wensum Sidings (Norwich) to Sheringham, Special Freight Train.*

Now this was to be a difficult one! As we go forward in time, after six years the fixed rail link had been removed from the road and the BR car park, the gates dismantled and scrapped and the linking track to NNR station, which was owned by BR, was removed. The signal box, of course, had been transferred to Platform 2 at the NNR station. I am never quite sure of the story here except that the local authority, who had realigned the road junction of Station Road and Station Approach, wanted the signal box out of the way as it was proving something of a hazard to visibility for road users. I think it was something of a political issue with BR wanting the council to do the work and the council saying it was BR's responsibility! It was also suggested that the North Norfolk Railway should contribute to the costs. The NNR had already purchased the lever frame and most of the remaining equipment including the gate wheel but the signal box itself was not included in the sale. This is where my memory eludes me! During the period between the new road alignments and the rescue of the equipment in the box, we moved the box off its base in rather a hurry almost certainly because our information was that it was to be demolished and we had not quite finished removing the equipment. We carefully secured the internal wooden part of the box using longitudinal timbers so that a crane could lift it off its base and lower it onto a lorry for the short journey to platform 2 where it remains to this day. The reason I cannot remember the details is that some 11 years later a BR official came to Sheringham about their signal box and called at the North Norfolk Railway. It was his job to check its structural condition. Being in some doubt about our acquisition we were perhaps a little economical with the truth and told him it had been removed years ago! He went away quite satisfied. I am still not sure if we own the box or inadvertently stole it!

Train Number 3 consisted of two ex "Brighton Belle" Pullman cars which were from a set of four stabled for a number of years at Manningtree, Essex. They were owned by the brewery giant Ind Coope Ltd who had plans to convert the Pullman cars into unique eating places, as add-ons to their public houses. Planning permission became an obstacle and they languished in the sidings deteriorating quite rapidly. We made an approach to Ind Coope for two of them on long term loan. Of the four coaches at Manningtree we selected just one of the second class open saloons and the motor-brake/saloon as the other. Later we were offered all four but our inspection confirmed the choice of two only as the remaining cars were in very poor condition. Although I am not sure of what happened to the remaining two there was talk that the owners of the "Orient Express" acquired them; certainly one of the cars in use today is referred to as being an ex- "Brighton Belle" vehicle.

There would be problems in transferring them to Sheringham as there was no suitable road access so at least part of their journey would, again, need to be by rail. After a relatively short time the two Pullman coaches were included in a Harwich to Norwich freight train. Another special train to Norwich had been organised which consisted of three suburban coaches which had been purchased from British Rail from the Cambridge area together with a 'PassFruit' goods van (intended to be used as a stores vehicle) which had travelled from Cambridge. Both trains were joined up at Wensum sidings in Norwich. The complete train was intended to travel as a 'fitted' freight train, 'fitted' meaning that all vehicles in the train were braked as opposed to 'unfitted' where the vehicles were without through-braking. There was a problem however as the two train sets had incompatible train braking systems; the Pullmans were air-braked and the other coaches vacuum-braked.

However this is jumping ahead. In planning the movements of the six vehicles we found that the cost of road transport from Norwich was huge with hauliers also refusing to handle one of the very heavy Pullman coaches – the motor coach weighing in at 70 tons. So this is when we started to think about a rail movement with the little problem that the level crossing rail link had been removed! Before the movements to Norwich had been organised we decided that we should examine the possibility of relaying a temporary crossing over the road. British Rail's Divisional Manager was rather 'surprised' at the suggestion and reminded us that such an operation would cost many thousands of pounds if BR did the work. We did not hesitate and offered to do all the work ourselves. Nothing like committing volunteers to a seemingly impossible task particularly as the work would have to be done between service trains finishing one day and starting again the next. Eventually British Rail agreed that we could do the work ourselves under the supervision of a BR Permanent Way Inspector.

This entailed several weeks of planning the operation which we called "Operation Coachbelle". We needed to apply for a Road Closure Order from the Highway Authority, which was granted after paying a fee and advertising our intentions in the local press. Train number 3 would run - we would re-lay the gap across the road!

We agreed with British Rail that the best time for the operation was after the last service train on Saturday evening and before the first service train on Sunday. At that time the first train on Sundays was about 2.00pm providing us with the longest period without other trains.

"Operation Coachbelle" meant starting work at 07.00 on Saturday with an expected finishing time about 04.00 on Sunday morning or more accurately, for a break and rest; it would be another fourteen hours before we finally finished. Many of the sixty-odd volunteers endured long shifts totalling 30 hours or more. Of course, there were many procedures to go through such as arranging road diversions and providing lighting for work at night etc. Much of the preparatory work for track laying towards the road was accomplished in the days preceding. This meant laying new track towards the road - a distance of about 300ft. In addition all the necessary stores of rails, sleepers, fishplates etc, for the actual crossing and the link to the BR line were placed near the road.

A special train needed to be assembled on the NNR side as the work involved removing not one but two buffer stops - the NNR line terminated at a buffer stop at the platform end as did the line from Cromer. This work was allocated to the ex Southern Region 12 ton hand-operated rail crane. This job alone needed four men on the winding handles as it took about half an hour just to raise the jib! The former Stewart & Lloyds Kitson-built steam locomotive "Colwyn" and diesel locomotive "Dr. Harry" provided the motive power for the numerous train movements. One reason for this was that it was thought important that sufficient light axle-load vehicles were available between the crane and the steam locomotive "Colwyn" so that the steam engine did not encroach on the rather delicate temporary road section.

The actual link totalled nearly 400 feet across council-owned land, the main road and through the BR car park. The preparation work for this stage started on time at 7.00am, "Colwyn" and "Dr. Harry" were busy making the various vehicle movements not only to make up the works train set but to shunt other vehicles to make enough room for the new arrivals.

In early afternoon volunteers started to dig up the BR car park as its level was some 18 inches above the rail levels on the BR side. A passageway had to be left for passengers on the BR DMU services who might have wondered why we were digging up the surface of the car park. It was hard work for the small team involved and they probably never gave a thought to the fact that they would also be involved in re-instating the car park the next day. As darkness approached at about 5.30pm, lighting equipment was moved into place and an hour later, when the road was officially closed to traffic, the area was well lit and the work of the temporary level crossing could start.

The rails and sleepers went on top of the road surface, keyed up and levelled with many bits of plywood, with ballast only used at the kerb ends where the road canted for drainage. This was soon followed by the track being extended to the buffer stop. After many weeks of planning nothing could now go wrong - alas at 10.30pm a crisis! We discovered that the lengths of rails which were the exact length of the buffer stop were no longer there! They were there when we started planning but not when we needed them.

This meant a hurried foray to Weybourne to find suitable rails and cut them to length. One of our regular volunteers and a great character, the late Peter Morris, accepted this job and incredibly he returned at about 1.30 am with rails somehow sticking out of his BMW!

By 2.30am (or to be accurate 3.30am as this was the night of all nights when the clocks changed) came the moment of truth as "Colwyn" and the 12 ton crane were to test the track. We dispensed with the idea of barrier vehicles between "Colwyn" and the hand crane as delicate positioning was necessary. The BR Inspector who paid us a night visit was satisfied with progress and suggested that our little locomotive would have no difficulty in crossing the temporary track in the road. A few creaks and groans but "Colwyn" moved into the middle of the road with no problem. It was however something of a shock for a few late night revellers suddenly confronted with a steam locomotive in the middle of Station Road.

All the work that could be done was done and many volunteers went away to get some well-earned rest and refreshments. We had to wait for the return of the BR Inspector before we could tackle the buffer stop but the crane was ready for the lift.

At 07.00, the same time as our special train departed Norwich, the BR Inspector supervised our lifting of the buffer stop which was parked to one side. Only the short gap remained. I don't know how many times the gap and the replacement rails were carefully measured by different people but the rails were still ¾" too long. Another crisis, but the BR Inspector took the matter in hand and simply closed up a number of expansion gaps on both the BR and newly laid line and in they dropped.

Finally, fifteen minutes late the first sighting of a BR brake-van heralded the approaching train propelled by another Brush type 31 Diesel. Very gently the diesel pushed the vehicle across the road onto the temporary track in the BR car park. "Colwyn" immediately steamed across the road and attached to them. With lots of whistles and cheers "Colwyn" hauled the six coaches into Sheringham station. All that needed to be done then was for "Colwyn" to make one more crossing to return the BR brake van to the waiting diesel and shunt in the crane to reinstate the buffer stop. It still took several hours for the clearing up process allowing Station Road to be reopened. The incredible "Operation Coachbelle" was over.

As a passing thought I have mentioned that BR officials realised that the train was made of stock with incompatible braking systems. The train was scheduled to be a 'fitted' freight train which means that brakes needed to be operational on all the vehicles. This was not the case, of course, as the 'Belle' coaches were air-braked and the other vehicles vacuum. A long way away in York higher officials tackled this by sending an air-braked guard's van from as far away as Stoke on Trent – a special train at that! All the guards vans in the eastern area were still fitted for vacuum braking at that time. The 'solution' was not of course a solution; the braking systems were still different! The York officials quickly realised their mistake and sent an immediate stop order for the train. This would have been a disaster for everyone but fortunately the wizened and experienced local BR official in charge knew the implications of postponing the trip and made sure he only got the stop order on Monday morning! He proudly told York that the stock had been delivered safely.

The events above can only give a brief summary of "Operation Coachbelle" described by many as the biggest largely volunteer operation ever undertaken on a heritage railway. They worked incredibly long hours sometimes in appalling weather conditions to complete this remarkable task.

The clearing up process was to take several hours but, of course, life for the citizens had to go on. The lady with the pram was one of many people who needed assistance from volunteers to cross the track. All were good humoured and welcomed the development of the North Norfolk Railway. Even though this was many years ago the town residents expressed regret that the North Norfolk Railway had lost a permanent connection with the national system. Many supported the idea of connecting the two railways at some future date!

*The week before Special Train No.3 much preparation work
took place to extend the current line towards the crossing.*

*Works trains were frequent during the preceding week with rails, sleepers and ballast made available for the temporary connecting line.*

*Work starts on digging up the BR car park as the surface was some nine inches above the rail level.*

*Fowler 0-4-0 diesel "Dr. Harry" on a works train unloading
track materials for constructing the connecting line.*

*The ex SR hand-operated crane busy removing the buffer stop which marked the end of NNR's current operations.*

*The ex SR crane loading and unloading materials
for the long working night ahead.*

*Track laying starts as night falls.*

*Through the late evening and as the weather
deteriorated, track laying continued.*

*2.30am as Kitson No.45 "Colwyn" positions the crane ready for lifting
the BR buffer stop. The local police keep an eye on what's happening!*

*The new dawn arrives as the BR buffer stop is lifted under the supervision of the BR Inspector. At the same time the special train was leaving Norwich for Sheringham.*

*NNR steam locomotive Kitson No. 45 "Colwyn" moves the SR hand crane into position over the temporary track.*

*The BR Inspector watches progress as the final sections are laid.*
*The weather changes for the worse with continuous snow.*

*This gives some idea of the number of volunteers involved. It was snowing*
*and very cold and news was that the special train had just left Norwich.*

*A crisis point. After much careful measurement the rails would not fit!*

*The BR Inspector takes over and following some
adjustments the rails are dropped in.*

*The railway link nearly completed.*

*On a foggy morning work was completed just as the
special freight train from Norwich approaches.*

*The BR diesel locomotive pushes the stock to the BR line limit ready for the NNR steam Locomotive "Colwyn" to take over.*

*The special train passes over the temporary level crossing*

*Colwyn' couples up to the special freight train.*

*'Colwyn' hauls the heavy train into Sheringham Station.*

*After placing the stock in the NNR sidings, "Colwyn" returns the
BR brake van to the waiting BR diesel-electric locomotive.*

*The temporary rails are removed to allow the BR buffer stop to be replaced.*

*After completing the train movements, the crane is placed in position to replace the BR buffer stop before the first passenger train arrives from Norwich.*

*The temporary rails are removed and carried back to
the NNR for loading onto a works train.*

*The works train assists by dragging rails from the crossing onto NNR property.*

*Life must go on for residents of Sheringham. Here a volunteer assists a lady with a pram over the temporary track.*

*Almost finished, the track lifted and the final advertising board replaced only minutes before the first service train was due to arrive*

# CHAPTER 5.

### *Other Special Freight Trains and a few*
### *Charter Trains to Sheringham (Halt.)*

"Operation Coachbelle" was very much a one-off project. A fourth special freight train was arranged to leave Norwich but this time the train terminated at Cromer (Beach) station. Again hauled by a diesel-electric Class 31 locomotive, it consisted of a former Sleeping Car, a fairly modern passenger coach known as a TSO (Tourist Second Open) and a suburban coach. For the onward movements to Sheringham the bodies of the coaches were lifted off by crane on to a low-loader and another lorry carried the bogies. The operation was carried out three times with the coaches re-assembled at Sheringham.

There were two more special trains relevant to the crossing but, of course, they did not actually cross to the North Norfolk Railway. The first was one of the famous High Speed Trains (HST) which are very rarely seen in Norfolk. In 1990 an HST charter train travelled from London (I think) to Sheringham Halt for the very first (and almost certainly the last) time. There were five crew members in the cab comprising the inspector, HST driver, conductor-driver and two other crew members leaning out of each cab door to guide the driver to 'kiss' the buffer stop! Some 200 passengers were aboard as the train approached the halt very slowly indeed and almost had to 'kiss' the buffer stop. This only allowed just one door of the eight coach train to open and one can imagine the time taken for the passengers to leave the train.

The second charter train was a hugely successful steam-hauled shuttle service from Norwich. Once again only part of one coach could fit on the platform making it a lengthy process for passengers to leave and join the train. Clearly the obvious solution of allowing charter trains into the much longer NNR platforms makes a great deal of sense.

It is worth noting too that the two charter trains mentioned are probably the only two such trains in over thirty years. Businesses in Sheringham can surely see the potential of the crossing and its occasional use. This means that charter trains carrying tourists will bring many extra visitors to Sheringham.

Another issue genuinely felt is that the crossing will spoil the lovely area known as "Ottendorf Green". This need not be the case as the following pictures show; similar tramways in other parts of the world have adapted short railway lines to provide very pleasing appearances. Apart from the actual rails there is little to show a railway line is there. The term 'tramway' in this instance is simply a technical term describing a railway without fencing.

*The first visit of a high speed train (HST) to Sheringham (Halt). The platform could only accommodate the front power unit and only one door section of the first coach from which nearly 200 passengers had to leave the train.*

*Ex LNER steam locomotive Class B1 No. 61264. The first steam hauled train in 45 years arrives at Sheringham (Halt) on a charter special. Photo: David Madden*

*Railway track can be made to fit into the environment. As the new link line crosses Ottendorf Green, the rails can be tastefully camouflaged by the surrounding surface area such as the grass being used on this tramway in Austria. Photo: David Madden.*

*The approaches to Mendoza Station, Argentina. Mendoza has a population of 800,000 but the railway system has been closed for many years. There are plans to re-open the line. The signals are beautifully preserved and show the British influence and the railway lines are embedded in trimmed lawns. Photo: David Madden*

*A Steelworks railway track in Germany embedded
in the road surface: David Madden*

# CHAPTER 6.

*Steve Ashling, Level Crossing Project Manager for
the North Norfolk Railway continues the story:*

It is October 2007 and Network Rail are having their annual Retirement
& Long Service Day at North Norfolk Railway. Taking advantage of
having senior Network Rail managers in Sheringham, Network Rail
Operations Manager and NNR Director, Steven Ashling, asked if he
would be permitted to string a temporary track across the road and run
a train over as a bit of stunt! The reply came back form the Regional
Director, "why not build a crossing?" The door was open! If the top
man thinks its worth doing then it is now or never.

Meetings were held between NNR and Network Rail, County
Highways and HM Railway Inspectorate. All said it could be done. The
latter added a caution in that unless the road traffic can be managed
better a full crossing would not be possible. However, an 'Occasional
use' tramway style crossing would be permitted. The rest of 2008 was
spent getting the necessary permissions and design work approved. In
May we held a Public Meeting and found that the town that said no to
Tesco were happy to accept our proposals. The only condition was that
we allow provision for the Christmas tree on the green, as the current
position would be in the four foot. This we would be happy to do. By
December 2008 we were ready to go. We had a small team comprising

Bob Wright working on the engineering, Julian Birley with fundraising and Steven Ashling with the operational side.

Surveys identified that most services would not be affected by our works but there is a British Telecom chamber to relocate and high voltage electric cables to lower. The former would cost £400k and would therefore kill the project dead. Fortunately, BT agreed to allow NNR to strengthen it in position. EDF's cables were just too shallow to remain in place and require moving at a cost of £25k.

Then comes the fundraising! We always knew that there was massive support for this project but when it comes to money that is another thing. At the time of writing, March 2009, this is proving to be a little slow and difficult at the present time. NNR have and are continuing to speak with Norfolk County Council and economic regeneration bodies to obtain financial support with little success. We are in no doubt that this project will benefit the town enormously by bringing in charter trains with a couple of hundred people on. By targeting these at the shoulders of the summer peak it can have the effect of lengthening the season. The 2009 50th anniversary gala in February demonstrated that a big event could fill the guesthouses, pubs and restaurants for miles around. In addition we are launching a fund raising campaign, inviting people to sponsor part of the crossing. This approach has been successful on other projects in the past, one can just hope that this will not be the exception. Asking for money in the current economic climate is understandably not easy. However, we have massive support from all stakeholders, the Councils and public alike so we know that if it can be funded it will be.

Sheringham Crossing is now a matter of when rather than if.

*David Madden*

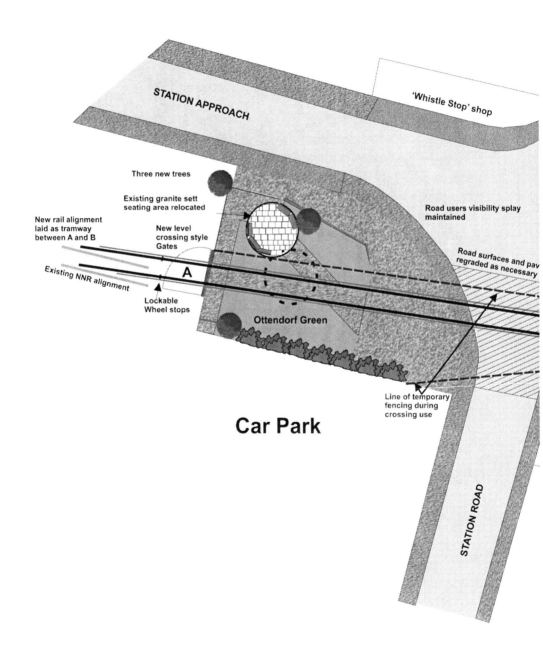

STATION APPROACH

'Whistle Stop' shop

Three new trees

Existing granite sett
seating area relocated

New rail alignment
laid as tramway
between A and B

New level
crossing style
Gates

Road users visibility splay
maintained

Existing NNR alignment

Road surfaces and pav
regraded as necessary

A

Lockable
Wheel stops

Ottendorf Green

Line of temporary
fencing during
crossing use

Car Park

STATION ROAD

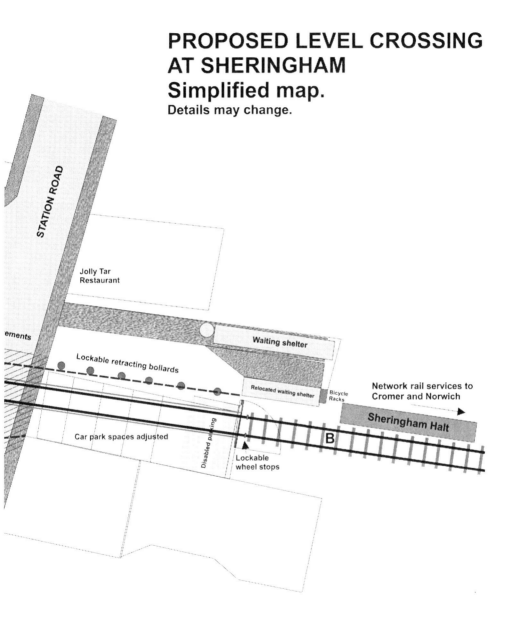

# PROPOSED LEVEL CROSSING AT SHERINGHAM
## Simplified map.
### Details may change.

STATION ROAD

Jolly Tar
Restaurant

ements

Waiting shelter

Lockable retracting bollards

Relocated waiting shelter

Bicycle
Racks

Network rail services to
Cromer and Norwich

Sheringham Halt

Car park spaces adjusted

Disabled parking

B

Lockable
wheel stops

Created from official drawings  by David Madden

# ACKNOWLEDGEMENTS

Brian Fisher for his superb photographs

David Morgan, Chairman, North Norfolk Railway Plc

The project team of Steven Ashling, Bob Wright and Julian Birley

David Harris, Chairman of the M&GN Society

Current and former editors of the M&GN Society' "Joint Line"

Retired employees of British Rail

Jill Wheatley who many times read and edited the drafts.

And to the many volunteers who have worked for the North Norfolk Railway.